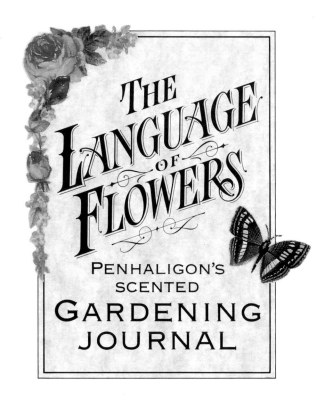

THE LANGUAGE OF FLOWERS

PENHALIGON'S SCENTED

GARDENING JOURNAL

THIS BOOK BELONGS TO

....

$\mathcal{I}$NTRODUCTION

Dear Gardener,

There is little more exciting than the planning of a new garden, whether it be a small patch waiting to be tilled before the vegetables are sown, or a large country garden, overgrown and in need of landscaping.

I have divided this Journal into different headings so that you may make your plans; some of them will be relevant to you, others will not. But rather like a garden where the plants spill over the borders with a life of their own, you may use the sections appropriate for your garden, overlapping into the rest.

When you are choosing the plants for a garden, I hope that you will think not only of the traditional requirements: type of soil, aspect, shape, colour and scent, but also of the meaning of the names of the plants in *The Language of Flowers*. In this way, you will always have flowers to pick that declare your love – roses, tulips, or forget-me-nots; flowers for friendship – rosemary, geraniums and bluebells; and flowers for children – primroses, lilies and daisies.

I have scented the pages of this Journal with *Violetta* to give you pleasure whilst you make your notes and to sustain you until you have cultivated your own sweet fragrances.

Sheila Pickles, London

CONTENTS

THE SPRING GARDEN

THE HERB GARDEN

FLOWERS FOR CUTTING

The Kitchen Garden

THE WILD GARDEN

The Cottage Garden

THE TERRACOTTA GARDEN

THE TOWN GARDEN

Beatrice Parsons

THE WALLED GARDEN

THE SUMMER GARDEN

THE SCENTED GARDEN

THE ROSE GARDEN

THE WATER GARDEN

The Italian Garden

THE TERRACE

The Herbaceous Border

The Arbour

The Lawn

The Autumn Garden

THE ORCHARD

FLOWERS FOR DRYING

TREES AND SHRUBS

THE CONSERVATORY

THE PARKLAND

Topiary

THE ORNAMENTAL GARDEN

The Winter Garden

Eugène Cligot. 1919.

THE GREENHOUSE

FAVOURITE GARDENS

Useful Addresses

Notes

A
GARDEN DIARY
YEAR PLANS

JANUARY

January

FEBRUARY

FEBRUARY

ARCH

MARCH

$\mathcal{A}$PRIL

APRIL

MAY

 MAY

JUNE

JUNE

July

 JULY

AUGUST

$\mathcal{A}$UGUST

SEPTEMBER

SEPTEMBER

OCTOBER

OCTOBER

November

November

DECEMBER

Compliments of the Season.

 DECEMBER

$\mathscr{A}$CKNOWLEDGEMENTS

The majority of illustrations were supplied by Bridgeman Art Library.
Additional material from: E. T. Archive; Fine Art Photographic
Library; Fitzwilliam Museum, Cambridge; Harris Museum & Art Gallery;
Private Collection; Royal Horticultural Society.

Cover: *Il Penseroso*, John Atkinson Grimshaw / Private Collection.
Back cover: *The Bunch of Lilacs*, James Jacques Tissot / Bridgeman Art Library.

$\mathscr{P}$ENHALIGON'S VIOLETTA

$\mathscr{T}$HE Language of Flowers stationery range has been scented for your pleasure with Violetta. The Victorians were very fond of violets and flower sellers with baskets full of the small purple bunches were a common sight on the streets of London.

Ever since the time of the Ancient Greeks the Violet has been recognized as something rare and desirable. That they are still in such demand today gives us an indication of the true worth of this modest flower with its powerful and distinctive scent.

If you would like more information on the Violetta range of products, or on Penhaligon's other ranges of perfumes and gifts, please contact : Penhaligon's, 41 Wellington Street, Covent Garden, London WC2. Telephone 071-836 2150.

Designed by Bernard Higton
Picture research by Lynda Marshall

Published by
HARMONY Books, a division of Crown Publishers, Inc.,
201 East 50th Street, New York, New York 10022

Published in Great Britain by
Pavilion Books Limited, London in 1992

HARMONY and colophon are trademarks of Crown Publishers, Inc.

Printed and bound in Italy by Arnoldo Mondadori

ISBN 0-517-58679-7

10 9 8 7 6 5 4 3 2 1

First American Edition